growing seeds!

Starting from Scratch

Linda D. Harris

Illustrations by Susan T. Fisher

FULCRUM PUBLISHING
GOLDEN, COLORADO

To Jesus Christ, creator of all seeds

Text copyright © 1999 Linda D. Harris
Illustrations copyright © 1999 Susan T. Fisher, Fisher Design
Cover image: "Oak seedling on white" by Steve Taylor/ Tony Stone Images

Library of Congress Cataloging-in-Publication Data
        Growing seeds : starting from scratch / Linda D. Harris ; illustrations by Susan T. Fisher.
            p. cm.
        Includes bibliographical references (p.) and index.
        ISBN 1-55591-395-4 (pbk.)
        1. Seeds.   2. Planting (Plant culture)   3. Gardening.   I. Title.
    SB321.H35   1999
    635'.0431—dc21   98-43317
                                                                    CIP

Printed in Thailand

0 9 8 7 6 5 4 3 2 1

Fulcrum Publishing
350 Indiana Street, Suite 350
Golden, Colorado 80401-5093
(800) 992-2908 • (303) 277-1623
website: www.fulcrum-gardening.com
e-mail: fulcrum@fulcrum-gardening.com

Table of Contents

Acknowledgments

Two good friends read this book when it was still young and gave me their valuable comments: Jan Allen, seed analyst, and Lynn May, horticulturist. Thank you!

Introduction

Hello! I wanted to write this collection of experiences and suggestions for you, because you're interested in plants and I'm glad you are! So please read through this book as you would a long letter from one gardening friend to another. It's not a textbook, but rather a notebook that I hope will encourage you to grow seeds. You're in for fun and sure success when you grow seeds.

I have worked for seed companies for many years, so I'm interested in seeds. Or perhaps it's the other way around. Seeds have never lost their charm for me, and what I hope to do is introduce you to that same fascination.

Seeds seem so simple, but they are not. Open up some seed packets and take a close look with a magnifying glass. There it is—the seed—dry, inert, small, rather drab in most cases. Every kind looks different, as do the plants that grow from them. You plant the seed, and it grows into the plant you expect. Simple!

Garden seeds will bring you much joy this year and every year you plant them. I hope this book gives you the information and confidence to grow seeds.

Chapter 1
What's in a Seed?

That little dry seed—how can it be alive? Planting a seed takes faith. Why? Because the seed stands for something that isn't yet. It's a promise. It's the future. What is awesome is its potential! To look at it, a seed is not impressive (although some are beautiful). But the wonder of a seed is all neatly packed inside.

What Is a Seed?

A seed is the fertilized, ripened ovule of a seed-producing plant, containing a living plant embryo capable of germinating and producing a new plant. That is a rather fancy way to describe it. More simply, a seed is the guarantee of another plant. It is even the guarantee of generations of plants! Because plants are specially designed to make seeds that will

Take a closer look at a seed.

ensure more plants like themselves, we know even before we plant it that the seed will grow. Nature counts on this assurance, and has for thousands of years. So I hope this certainty will give you confidence in the ability of a seed to grow.

Seed Physiology

As a flower is pollinated and seeds form within the drying flower, certain structures form within each seed. In this way a seed is just like a baby animal or human, with tiny specialized parts that will function as soon as they are needed.

A tiny living plant embryo rests suspended inside each seed. This ability to wait suspended is called "viability," sometimes "longevity," which refers to its lasting vitality. Some seeds have a long viability when kept perfectly dry (beans, 5 years or more). Some seeds have a short viability. The reasons for the sleeping state are that the seeds do not begin to grow while still inside the parent flower, and they don't start growing just after being dispersed from it. If each seed started to grow immediately, it would compete with the parent plant nearby and be choked out. In seeds of annual plants (plants that grow, bloom, and set seeds all in 1 year), the seeds are programmed to grow the following season. Why? Because the next season will present the most favorable conditions for germination, and a long growing season—in which the plant can fully develop—will be a certainty. Nature doesn't like to waste its precious resources.

Cotyledons

Seed Coat

Hypocotyl

Radicle

Endosperm

Hilum

Cross section of a bean seed, showing internal structures.

The Visible Seed

Around the outside of a seed is the seed coat, a protection against injury and moisture loss. Just inside is the endosperm (stored food source) and the cotyledons. Nestled down inside that is the embryo. The embryo has a radicle with a root cap, and a shoot with a tiny foliage leaf and growing tip.

Germination

How do seeds know when to grow? In some cases a seed can stay in a sleeping state for years, healthy and viable, waiting for the right conditions. Everything inside a seed is programmed and ready to grow when certain conditions are met. This happens when the seed is planted.

"Germination" is the fancy term for the sprouting and development of a seed. When a seed comes in contact with soil and moisture, it begins to absorb (imbibe) water and oxygen. Germination is a very busy time within a seed. Imbibed water and oxygen activate enzymes that stimulate the seed to resume activity. Cells begin to divide and differentiate. This is called growth.

A seed uses the water it absorbs, and oxygen from the water or air surrounding it, plus its own stored energy from the endosperm that was provided when it formed, for the strength required to unfurl and push its developing structures outward and into the soil.

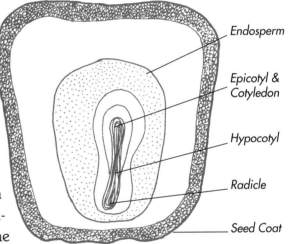

Endosperm

Epicotyl & Cotyledon

Hypocotyl

Radicle

Seed Coat

Cross section of a corn seed, showing internal structures.

The first cell division begins in the radicle. As cells grow and divide, the radicle elongates, pushing itself and its protective root cap out through the seed coat and into the soil. It forms root hairs, which absorb water and minerals from the soil.

As the cells divide and grow, the next structure to develop is the hypocotyl, the first "stem," at the top of which are the two cotyledons. In some seeds there is only one cotyledon such as grass, corn, and wheat. The hypocotyl elongates and begins to bend, pulling the cotyledons from the seed coat. As the cotyledons absorb moisture, they expand and push the seed coat off until it falls away from the new plant.

Then the tiny shoot, the epicotyl, begins to elongate and grow upward toward the light, using the strength of stored food in the cotyledons and the water and solutes supplied by the root hairs. The new plant unfurls its first true leaves and begins making its own food by photosynthesis.

As the second and third pairs of leaves form, the cotyledons have shriveled and will fall off. Voila! Independent life and growth, and a new plant with the ability to produce seeds.

That little dry seed is alive! I'll bet you can't wait to get started and see what it will do.

Chapter 2

Getting Started

You've probably never thought about the information on the back of a seed packet. Somebody actually writes that stuff! So take a look at it—you may even want to save it for reference later. Keep your empty packets in an old card file box. It's fun to look at them in seasons to come.

Seed packets: instructions in miniature.

Seed Packets

Of course you need some seed packets to get started growing your own seeds. But you also need the basic information given on the backs of most seed packets. In a "kernel" it gives you just what you need to know to plant your seeds.

Growing Seeds!

The packet indicates suggested spacing between seeds, the spacing between rows, the planting depth (amount to cover the seeds), and the approximate number of days until the seed germinates. This information is a good guideline to follow, but you don't have to do everything exactly. The only measurement you should be strict about is the amount of soil used to cover the seeds. *Don't cover them more deeply than instructed.* With very small seeds, you can simply press them down into the soil and leave them uncovered.

Seed packets may indicate the average number of days until the seeds will result in a plant that blooms or produces. When you look at this number, don't take it as "cast in concrete." It's just a guide so you know what to expect if your plant grows in the most perfect conditions. In northern gardens, maturity dates (days to produce the vegetable) can be 1 or 2 weeks later than stated on the packet—just because of cool spring weather. This number means the days from planting the seed until the first flower or vegetable appears (if the directions are for planting outdoors); when the planting directions are for "starting seeds indoors," this maturity figure means the days from when you plant your small seedlings outdoors until they bloom or produce the first flower or fruit. There's quite a difference there.

On a seed packet, you'll usually find a description of the mature plant, and sometimes a picture showing what the plant will look like when it's grown. Also notice the weight of the seeds inside (and sometimes the number of seeds inside). Although I usually pay no attention to how many seeds I get in a packet, a lot of folks do. The cost of the seeds is the very lowest cost of anything else you need for your garden, so why fuss about how many? Get an extra packet and plant them both! You're probably thinking, "Well sure, she works for a seed company!" But when I plant seeds, I want a lot of seedlings. Even if I buy two packets, it's still not costing me very much, and I'll have more seedlings than I need.

Containers

Containers for seed starting don't have to be fancy. They should be sterile, though. You can reuse old plastic or clay pots if you soak and scrub them first in a solution of one part bleach to ten parts water. Let them dry before you fill them with planting mixture. I like peat pots and peat pellets. They're inexpensive, sterile, and biodegradable in the garden. Pressed paper "packs" and trays are useful, too. Some folks who like to recycle use paper milk cartons they have cut short. One thing that's not good for starting seeds is an egg carton; because the cells are so shallow, there's not much room for the seedling roots to develop well. Instead, use anything that holds at least 2 inches of soil mixture. Styrofoam coffee cups are great.

Poke a hole in the bottom of each container so that excess water can drain. Fill the containers with sterile seed-starting mixture. Or, if you use peat pellets, you don't need the mixture at all. The pellets are all ready to go.

Seed-Starting Mixtures

Please use a soil mixture that is sterile or sterilized when you grow seeds indoors. Why? Because you are trying to give seeds their optimum growing conditions, the soil you use for planting should be free of disease organisms and microscopic critters. If you use soil straight from your garden, you don't really know what's in it. You may unknowingly be introducing a disease or insect into your seed-starting soil.

Instead, use a potting soil marked "For Seed Starting" and make sure it says "sterile" or "sterilized" on the bag. Some of these mixtures actually contain no real "soil" at all, but consist of peat moss and vermiculite or perlite. Some have fertilizer added.

Another reason to use this kind of soil is that it's light in texture. When you cover your seeds, they will not be buried too deeply, and light can penetrate through to the seeds. This kind of mixture also allows perfect drainage and air circulation around the tiny roots. I hope I've convinced you. Why not start with the very best conditions—you want healthy seedlings, don't you?

If you want to make your own mix, there's a recipe on page 68.

Tools and Supplies

You'll need some sort of waterproof tray. I've used dishpans, washbasins left over from hospital stays, old lasagna pans, cake pans, cat litter trays, and actual seedling trays; they're all fine. Some are just prettier than others.

Have you ever heard of a "dibble"? It's a great word and fun to say. And folks will look at you a little funny when you say it.

A dibble is a tool with a pointed end, like a large awl. It can be as fancy as an aluminum point with an oak T-shaped handle, or as simple as an old pencil stub (point not required). I prefer the pencil. You can even use a trowel. A dibble is useful both for gently lifting clumps of seedlings before you transplant them and for making a hole in the soil and placing the seedling in it. Keep one around in your seed-starting stuff.

My favorite dibble is an old pencil.

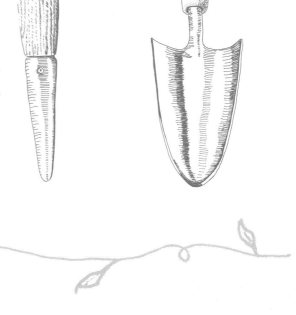

Another handy tool is an old bucket or large old paint can with a handle. In it you can keep all your seed-starting stuff so you always know where everything is, plus it's easy to haul around.

Marking stakes—whether old popsicle sticks or white plastic plant stakes about 4 inches long—are important when you're growing several different kinds of plants from seeds.

Write on them with a pencil—it will not fade or wash off. Add a pencil with a point to your bucket.

About marking stakes with seed packets: I wouldn't if I were you. A few rain showers will make your packet into a soggy mess, and a few weeks of hot sun will fade it so you can't read it anyway. Keep them indoors somewhere if you think you'll want to look at them again. They make great references, both for this season and in the future.

Try using a plant light. A simple shop light on a chain, with fluorescent fixtures, will work fine for growing healthy seedlings indoors. You'll also need a mister bottle and a watering can with a sieve on the end.

Sources for Supplies

Check out the garden department of your local big retailer, hardware store, large florist, craft and plant store, or garden center. Garden centers are my favorite place to look for supplies because they have a wide selection of stuff for seed starting. There's usually a choice, whereas at retailers there is generally only one kind of thing you're looking for. And garden centers carry these items all year long, unlike some of the large retail stores.

Another great source for seed-starting supplies is mail-order catalogs. Many of these companies offer great products that you may not be able to find locally. It's worth the shipping fee (and sometimes there's no shipping fee) to get soil mixtures and pots by mail, because you don't have to go all over the place looking for one thing here and one thing there. You get the picture. For a list of mail-order seed and plant catalogs, many of which have seed-starting supplies, check the

Internet. Here's a good place to start: http://www.gardennet.com. You can also shop directly on the Internet. Just do a search for "seeds" and lots of companies will come up for you to investigate.

Planning and Timing

Timing your seed growing is an important aspect of success. Get yourself an inexpensive notebook—or use the back pages of this book—to make notes. You'll keep these notes and refer to them year after year.

A seed gardener must learn to count backward. In winter or early spring, start with your last spring frost date (see Chapter 5) and count back the number of weeks the seed packet suggests. This gives you the date for planting, whether indoors or out. But who wants to do this every year? I hate math, so I just make a note to myself for next winter: when to start things indoors (by name) and about when to plant seeds outdoors (by name). In the summer, count backward from your first fall frost to find the best time to start seeds of fall vegetables. Whenever this is, it's usually a good time to plant perennial and biennial flower seeds, too. You'll find a sample chart like this on pages 69–70.

One mistake many folks make when starting seeds indoors is doing so too early. For instance, tomato seeds need to be started 6 to 8 weeks before you will set them outdoors in the garden. Yet you can't plant them outdoors in the ground until spring frost is over. Say you are in Zone 6, where the last spring frost is about May 15. Counting backward from there, March 20–April 3 is about the right time to start.

Add another week for germination, and you have the indoor planting date for your tomatoes: March 13–March 20. If you start them in January, as some folks do in their excitement and desire for spring, what happens? You get plants that really want to be outside but can't because of the weather. They need bigger and bigger pots, and get taller and taller. It can be tricky keeping these plants healthy indoors and giving them the continuous bright light, water, temperature, and nutrients they need until their outdoor planting date arrives. If you have a greenhouse, no problem. But if not, wait longer; you'll have better results when plant management is a new experience for you.

Chapter 3
What Seedlings Need

Plant Processes

As a grower of seeds, you are really a plant manager. The following information will help you understand why good management produces good plants. When you know a plant's processes, you can provide exactly what your seedlings (baby plants) require to grow and mature normally. You need to understand the following factors—the *why*—to be a good plant manager. Read on—science is fun!

How Plants Grow

Does the same part of a plant move upward as a plant grows? It looks that way if you watch a bean seedling grow in your garden. But actually the only place growth occurs is in the very tips of the plants, whether that part is aboveground or below the soil. New cells are formed there, which elongate and mature. This is called "growing." But once the cells have formed, they themselves don't move upward or outward. Only the new growth at the tips of the shoots and at the tips of the roots is actually moving (growing) by making new cells.

When you understand that it is the seedling's job to grow new cells at its top and bottom tips, and to do so continuously without interruption, then you understand the reason for providing the best conditions you can—continuously—so the seedlings can reach their potential.

Plant Parts

ROOTS

Plants have at least as much of a root system as they have growth aboveground. In some studies, root systems have been measured, and some have been found to have miles of roots! Healthy roots are essential for plant growth and function.

Provide even moisture for your seedlings.

The root is the first part of a seedling to emerge from the seed. The first root (called a radicle) is covered with tiny hairs that begin to absorb water from the surrounding soil while anchoring the plant in place. At the very tip of the root, cells are produced by dividing, and as they enlarge and elongate, the root cap is pushed through the soil. New root hairs are formed along the new growth of each root, and it is their function to absorb water, providing a continuous supply of moisture to the plant. Water is required to enable the seed to unfurl its already formed cotyledons and stems and emerge above the ground.

STEM AND LEAVES

As the cells divide and the stem and cotyledons unfurl, they are pushed (like the root cap) upward into the air and light. The stem raises the cotyledons upward. These cotyledons, the first leaves on a seedling, are structures formed within the seed. They are often seed-shaped, and usually look nothing like the "true" leaves of the plant, which will develop and follow shortly. They are usually thick and fleshy because they are a storage organ for the seedling, containing nutrition in a handy package to keep the seedling growing strongly. The stem continues to expand and grow upward. Above the cotyledons is the growing tip, and from that tip grows a set of true leaves. You'll usually see the cotyledons start to wither and yellow and then drop off because they have been "used up."

The Environment

Light

Plants are energy factories—they make their own food from the sunlight and sustain themselves completely by their own processes. Plants are the only living beings that can convert solar energy into chemical energy (their "food"). Therefore sunlight is essential to plant growth.

Plants convert solar energy into food in their leaves by a process called photosynthesis. It's carried out in special leaf cells containing chlorophyll, which is what gives plants their green color. The food produced consists of sugars, starches, minerals, and so on in solution, and is then transported from the leaf throughout the entire plant.

Water

Plants are made up mostly of water—over 75 percent in most plants. Water is essential for plant health and growth. How does water act inside a plant?

There are special structures for water inside every plant. Called the vascular system, it is composed of tiny tubelike conduits, somewhat like our own veins and arteries, which allow water to be absorbed and conducted throughout the plant. There are special tubes for water and nutrients (called xylem), and others for transporting solutes (food), called phloem. In a tiny seedling, all these structures are already formed. They are very small and delicate, as you can imagine, so never pick up a seedling by its stem! You could accidentally crush part of the vascular system. This is so important I've mentioned it elsewhere in this book. Instead, pick up a seedling (when you are transplanting it) by a leaf—it can always grow another leaf if that one becomes damaged, but if the stem is damaged, healing or replacement is not always possible.

Nutrients

Do seedlings need fertilizer? Not right away. Seeds have some energy stored within them (in the cotyledons), enough to get the seedling going for several weeks.

NPK is the nutrition code for gardeners. These are the three most important elements in a fertilizer and are required for healthy plant growth. The letters represent each nutrient's chemical symbol on the periodic table of the elements.

N = Nitrogen. The first number in a string of three numbers separated by hyphens on a fertilizer label. Nitrogen is a chemical needed for fast, sturdy growth of stems and leaves. The number represents the percentage of available nitrogen in the fertilizer formula.

P = Phosphorus. The second number in the string. Phosphorus is needed for healthy growth of roots. The number represents the percentage of available phosphorus in the fertilizer formula.

K = Potassium (a.k.a potash). The third number in the string. Potassium is a chemical required by plants for healthy production of flowers and fruit. The number represents the percentage of available potassium in the fertilizer formula.

You can already get the idea that a balance of chemicals is the secret to plant nutrition and health. A plant's nutritional needs are like ours, in a way. A balance of nutrients is necessary, and if they are not available, the evidence of any deficit will become apparent after a while.

Space

Plants need room to grow. This sounds so obvious it's almost stupid to say! But when we plant seeds, we sometimes forget how big the plants will actually become, and seedlings grow fast. If plants are too close together, they compete with each other for sunlight, water, and nutrients. We normally don't see what happens to roots under these conditions, but it's painfully apparent when the seedling's top growth begins stretching and turning pale green. When your plants start stretching for light, they are weak and wobbly. This puts them at a great disadvantage for healthy growth later. How to avoid this? Allow the suggested spacing between each plant for the best results in fruits and flowers.

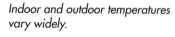

Indoor and outdoor temperatures vary widely.

Temperature

When you plant seeds, you want them to germinate quickly, so the soil needs to be warm. We're talking about soil temperature. But after the seedlings have emerged, you want their growth to be slow but steady. This is best achieved when the air temperature is not too high. When the air temperature is about right (65–70 degrees F in daytime, 60 degrees F at night), the growth of cells is continuous, with strong cell walls and normal cell size. When the air temperature is too high, growth is accelerated, which is not good because the cell walls are not as strong as they would be under cooler temperatures. Cells become too large. What happens then? You'll have weak-stemmed seedlings that can barely stand upright. It's hard (and sometimes impossible) for the little things to recover from this state of weakness. You want to have healthy seedlings!

Chapter 4
Planting Seeds Outdoors

Why Plant Seeds Directly Outdoors?

Planting (or "sowing") seeds directly outdoors in the garden is the easiest way to grow seeds. This is how nature does it, and it has been a successful method for thousands of years. Why reinvent the wheel? However, the knowledge (or confidence) required to plant seeds outside seems to be a mysterious art or a lost art because it is so easy to buy started plants today. Started plants are okay, but they are only available in the spring, and the selection of varieties is often quite limited.

Since I have had great results with seeds planted directly outdoors, I hope to dispel the mystery and get you started planting seeds outdoors, too. So here is the best advice I can pass along: Plant your seeds outdoors, where they are to grow, for the best possible results. Why?

Growing Seeds!

- Seeds planted outside (at the best time for the seed) are subject to natural fluctuations in temperature, light, and moisture, so they grow more slowly and are much sturdier.
- Seedlings don't get disturbed later by transplanting, or by being crowded in a tiny pot, so their roots are stronger.
- They grow faster and bloom just as early as seedlings started indoors.
- You can have lots and lots of plants from one packet of seeds. It's a much more economical way to garden, so you can grow a lot more different kinds without spending very much.

There is nothing comparable to the satisfaction of raising your own plants from seed and having them bloom and produce. It will give you an essential ownership and interest you will never feel about store-bought plants.

How to Plant Seeds Outdoors

Make a sketch of the garden area. Draw in roughly where you want to plant each type of seed.

The seed packet will tell you whether sun or shade is required for each plant you grow. Most plants—flowers and vegetables—grow best in sun. Choose a sunny area where the soil drains well after a rain. "Full sun" means an area that receives sunshine all day, without shadows falling over it.

In spring, wait until the soil has dried enough so that a clump of soil pressed in your palm falls apart when you release your fingers. This is descriptively called the "clump test." If you dig in soil that is still too wet and sticky, it can damage the soil structure and cause growing problems for your plants. So wait—the soil will be a little warmer, too, which is good for the seeds.

If this is a new garden area, test your soil with a home soil test kit or have the County Extension Service do it for you (they provide low-cost and dependable results). The soil test will tell you whether any nutrients or adjustments are required, and how much to add. Please don't guess! It's better not to add anything than to add too much. Most soils are already full of nutrients that plants need for growth.

Prepare the soil. Dig with a fork or spade down 8 to 12 inches, loosening and turning the soil. Continue until the whole area has been loosened. Add peat moss, composted leaves, composted horse or cow manure, or other organic material. Mix it all together and smooth the soil surface with a rake.

Plant your seeds as suggested on the packet. Cover them lightly with loose soil, or simply press them into the soil. The most common reason that seeds fail to come up is that they've been planted too deep. Many seeds need light to germinate. Scatter the seeds very thinly. A good way to do this is to empty the whole seed packet into your palm. Pick up small pinches with your other hand and sprinkle them over the area.

Broadcast, Bands, or Rows?

Most seed packets give directions to plant seeds in a row. This is a good way to do it if you are new at planting seeds. Mark the row with a popsicle stick or plastic stake so you know where to look for your new seedlings. When they come up, they'll be easy to spot from surrounding weedlings because they'll all be in a straight line. This is a good way to learn to identify seedlings by sight. Otherwise you may pull some of them up by mistake, thinking they are weeds! In a band is a great way to plant radish, lettuce, carrot, and beet seeds. The band is just a very wide row, 3 to 6 inches across. Mark it with a stake so you'll know about where to expect your seedlings to appear. Broadcasting seeds is a great method, too—the one I usually use, because each seed has plenty of room to grow and the need to thin the seedlings later is lessened. Broadcast directions are provided mostly for flower mixtures and lawn grass, but you can plant almost any seeds this way.

Keep the soil evenly moist until seedlings appear. Use a watering can with a sprinkler sieve. Protect your seeds from washing away in heavy rains by applying a light mulch of peat moss or salt hay, if desired. I usually don't cover my seeds this way, but later I look all around the area carefully for seedlings that may appear somewhere else than where I planted them. (Dig 'em up carefully and move 'em— or change your garden to accommodate the serendipity!)

When seedlings have several pairs of leaves, cut off the weaker and smaller ones with household scissors, so the plants are spaced as suggested on the seed packet. Leave the seedlings with the thickest stems. You may hate to do this, but it is the secret to healthy growth and flowering. Be ruthless and cut! (That's why I recommended sowing the seeds very thinly over the area. You won't have so many to cut off.)

Water the small plants gently, and keep watering regularly as they grow. Many gardeners fertilize their flowers, but most annuals bloom best if grown "hungry." Perennial flowers and bulbs should have a low-nitrogen fertilizer once in spring or fall. Vegetables do need fertilizer. Sprinkle a balanced fertilizer over the soil when you are preparing it, then plant. Balanced fertilizer contains the three elements: nitrogen, phosphorus, and potassium. Or fertilize with a liquid fertilizer solution as suggested on the label. Fertilize vegetable plants again around July 1.

Control the weeds for best results, so that your planted plants won't have wild "weedlings" sucking up their water and nutrients. Some folks like to mulch around plants after they've started to grow well, which discourages weeds between plants. For mulch, use peat moss in a layer about 1 inch deep. This is a great way to conserve soil moisture, too. But I prefer pulling my weeds by hand, one by one—it's great therapy for stress—so my gardens have the "bare soil" look. But if you don't have much time to weed, use a mulch.

Outdoor Containers

You can also plant seeds directly into large patio containers, barrels, or hanging baskets.

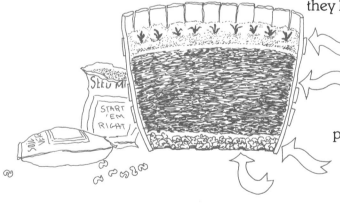

First year: Use the largest containers you can afford. Make sure they have drainage holes in the bottom. Put a layer of gravel or foam packing peanuts in the bottom of each container. Fill the containers with a mixture of garden soil and peat moss or leaf compost, and perlite or vermiculite. On the very top layer, use an inch or two of pure seed-starting mix. Plant your seeds as already described, and follow the same steps. Take special care to thin plants so they have room to grow well. It just makes sense—you'll have only a few plants in a container. After your plants get larger, check the pots every day. If the soil feels dry on top, water. Water your containers every day, or more often when the weather is very hot and dry. This is especially important for hanging baskets because they dry out quickly and may need watering more than once a day.

Second year: Replace most of the soil (or at least the upper half) with a seed-starting mix for best results. Then replant your pots.

Cold Frames

A cold frame extends your growing season by providing a sheltered growing area. Using a cold frame for seedlings is a method halfway between planting indoors and planting outdoors, a kind of paradise for seedlings. Seeds planted in a cold frame germinate very well. Seedling roots go down unrestricted into the ground, and their top growth is sturdy because of bright light and outdoor air temperatures. Here is a list of plants that are good for cold frame growing:

- **Annual flowers:** pansy, aster, calendula, stock, snapdragon, larkspur
- **Perennial flowers:** delphinium, lupine, carnation
- **Biennial flowers:** lunaria, sweet william, wallflower
- **Perennial and biennial herbs:** (especially parsley and chives)
- **Cole crops:** Cauliflower, cabbage, brussels sprouts
- **Leafy Crops:** Lettuce and other salad greens
- **Root Crops:** Onions, leeks, radishes

A cold frame is very simple to make. You can use cinder blocks or bricks for the frame. For the top, use a large piece of framed glass, such as an old window sash or French door, or a sheet of translucent fiberglass. Dig an area of soil, then build the frame to fit the top you've chosen. The sides should be 12 to 24 inches above the soil. Some folks like to make the back higher than the front. The top need not be fastened to the frame. You'll need several props to hold the top open during the warm parts of the day. Place your cold frame on the south or west side of the house or garage, where it is not shaded by trees.

Or you can buy a specially designed polycarbonate cold frame and get an automatic vent opener, which is very handy if you're not around the house all day.

Winter: Depending on your climate, you may be able to grow salad greens, green onions, and radishes all through the winter. A mulch of weed-free hay is helpful around plants in the cold frame during northern winters. The important thing is to ventilate the cold frame on sunny days—if the top remains closed, temperatures can really soar in there. Prop open the lid some, so air can flow in and out. Open the frame in midmorning and close it in late afternoon. Brush snow off the top.

Early spring: Start your cole crops, onions, and perennial herbs for later transplanting to the garden. Plant perennial and biennial flower seeds and the seeds of the annual flowers just listed.

Mid- to late summer: Start your cole crops for fall, perennial and biennial herbs, perennial and biennial flowers, and pansies in the frame (you won't need the lid until fall temperatures drop low at night), and winter the plants over (let them grow on) in the frame. This extra protection assures you of sturdy plants to transplant to the garden in the spring when garden soil can be worked. Your frame-grown pansies will really thrill you! And summer-started perennials usually bloom faster than spring-planted perennials.

Notes

Chapter 5
Planting Seeds Indoors

Which, Why, and How?

*I*f you want to grow seeds indoors, choose those that really benefit from a little extra time and attention. Some seeds need an indoor head start, because they are slow to germinate, slow-growing, love heat, or have very tiny seeds. By starting these seeds indoors, you can have better control over their germination and growth (good management). Here's a list:

- Tomato, pepper, eggplant
- Impatiens
- Petunia
- Specialty blooming plants such as cyclamen, cineraria, and calceolaria
- Tropical plants such as banana, bird-of-paradise, and cactus

Growing Seeds!

Fun plants for growing indoors: African violet, herbs, coleus, other houseplants

When growing vegetable and flower seeds, you will be growing the seedlings indoors for only a few weeks and then transplanting them to the garden. When you grow seeds indoors, you need to create an environment that mimics Nature. Bright light and uniform moisture are the most crucial requirements for healthy seedlings. If you do this right, you'll have healthy seedlings every time!

Soil and Pots

Use peat pots or pellets for the best results. They're inexpensive, sterile, and biodegradable in the garden. Fill the pots with sterile seed-starting mixture (see sidebar).

Sow seeds according to the seed packet directions, barely covering them or just pressing them into the soil. In a 3-inch pot, plant three to five seeds—fewer seeds if they are larger than tomato seeds, and more if they are smaller than tomato seeds. When you have finished planting, place your planted pots or pellets in a leakproof tray filled with about 1 inch of water. Let them stay in the tray until they are completely saturated with water (the surface will turn dark), usually several hours.

Now place the tray under lights (see next section) and under normal room temperature. My favorite trick to get seedlings to germinate quickly is to place the

About Seed-Starting Mixture

Please use a soil mixture that is sterile or sterilized when you grow seeds indoors. Why? Because you are trying to give seeds their optimum growing conditions, the soil you use for planting should be free of disease organisms or microscopic critters. If you use soil straight from your garden, you don't really know what's in it. You may unknowingly introduce a disease or insect into your seed-starting soil.

Instead, use a potting soil marked "For Seed Starting" and make sure it says "sterile" or "sterilized" on the bag. Some of these mixtures actually contain no real "soil" at all, but consist of peat moss and vermiculite or perlite. Some have fertilizer added. Another reason to use this kind of soil is that it's light in texture. When you cover your seeds, they will not be buried too deeply and light can penetrate through to the seeds. This kind of mixture also allows perfect drainage and air circulation around the tiny roots. Why not start with the very best conditions so you get healthy seedlings?

tray *on top of* the fluorescent light fixtures with the lights on. The low amount of heat from the fixture produces "bottom heat," which is preferred by many seeds (pepper, eggplant, impatiens), and it gets them up and growing surprisingly fast.

Light

Although sunlight is the best light for plants, it's difficult to provide enough bright sunlight indoors. When sunlight comes through glass windows, it loses some of its brightness. Light intensity is measured in foot-candles. Just a foot or so away from the window, the light intensity is a great deal lower. Since seedlings need constant, bright light, I use fluorescent lights. It need not be a fancy light tube made for plants. Plain cool-white fluorescent tubes are fine. A shop light works wonderfully. Or, for more aesthetic appeal, get yourself a tabletop plant light or a plant cart with fluorescent light fixtures.

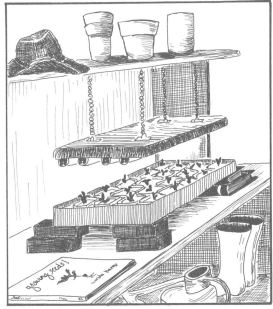

Hang lights 6–8 inches above the tops of plants.

IMPORTANT: When you place your planted pots and seedlings under the lights, they should be only 6 to 8 inches below the tubes. As the plants grow, either raise the lights or lower the seedlings (whichever is easier) so the plants maintain this distance from the lights. I turn the lights on in the morning, leave them on 12 to 18 hours a day, and turn them off at night.

Growing Seeds!

Care

WATERING

Keep the soil around your seedlings evenly moist. Do not let them dry out! If you have to be away during their early growth, get a friend to stop by and water. It may be easiest to water from the bottom when seedlings are very small. Pour water in the tray and let it be soaked up from below.

TEMPERATURE

As already explained, "bottom heat" is good for germination. Soil temperatures at 70–75 degrees F are appreciated by most indoor seeds. The idea is to get them up quickly. Once the seedlings are up, however, cooler air temperatures are a must. Why? The sturdiness of your seedlings is directly related to cool air temperatures, which allow slower, sturdier growth the way it would occur in nature. Ideal air temperatures for indoor seedlings are 70–75 degrees F in daytime, 60–65 degrees F at night.

TOUCHING

Am I crazy? No, actually there is some research to support this suggestion. Brush across the tops of your seedlings with your fingers or palm daily. What does this accomplish? Sturdier stems—and more interest on your part. Honest.

FERTILIZING

The soil or planting medium you use will supply some nutrients to the seedling. Some seed-starting soil mixtures contain fertilizer just strong enough for small seedlings. So don't worry about supplying additional nutrients until about the fifth or sixth week. In many cases the seedlings are going to be planted outdoors at about this age. To fertilize at this point, use a liquid solution (water with a little fertilizer added). You can mix any of the following with water in a watering can or mister bottle: crystallized plant food such as Miracle Gro, RapidGro, or Peters, or liquid plant food such as Schultz or fish emulsion. Use the amount suggested *for seedlings*. If this is not given, use *half* the amount suggested for mature plants. Dissolve the fertilizer completely in water. Pour it gently around the seedlings, or spray it on the seedlings and soil surface in place of plain water. Use it for every watering until you set the plants out in the garden. The same fertilizer solution should be used when transplanting (see following section). If you're growing vegetables, continue to water newly planted seedlings for several weeks with this solution. If I'm growing flowers, I don't bother with fertilizer after plants are established. I have found that most flowers bloom better when "hungry."

THINNING

When are they "done"? It's not a size, it's a stage of growth. When your seedlings have several pairs of true leaves, they need more room. It's time to thin them out.

Cut off weaker and smaller seedlings at soil level using household scissors, leaving one per 3-inch pot. You may hate to do this, but it is the secret to healthy growth. Be ruthless.

Okay, okay—if you really want to save them all, with a pencil or plastic spoon (your dibble), gently lift up the whole clump of seedlings in the pot. Holding them *by the leaves, not the stem*, carefully separate and repot each one in its own pot or pellet. This is called pricking out.

There, now, you have way more than you need. Give some away!

Keep your plants growing under lights until about a week before your last expected spring frost (see sidebar on page 37).

HARDENING OFF

This is a funny-sounding term, but it's a perfect description for the process of helping your indoor-grown seedlings to adjust to life outdoors. Do it gradually, over a week or two.

Your pampered darlings have been growing indoors under almost perfect temperatures with regular watering and artificially supplied light. Hardening them off will allow them to gradually accustom themselves to the "real world"—fluctuating temperatures, light, moisture levels, and wind, which will affect their growth in the garden.

A week or so before your outdoor planting date, take your seedlings outdoors in a tray or box, and put them *in the shade* for a few hours that first day. Bring them indoors and resume their indoor care. The next day, increase their time outdoors by a few more hours. On the following day, give them dappled sun and make sure they don't dry out. It's amazing how fast a small peat pot can dry out. Gradually expose the seedlings to more and more sun and longer hours outdoors until they're staying out overnight. If the plants are frost-tender, protect them with a cover at night if the temperature drops to 40 degrees F or

below. You'll notice that your seedlings seem to have stopped growing. They are toughening their cell walls to stand upright and sturdy in the garden.

Transplanting to the Garden

The best time to transplant your seedlings is on a cloudy day. If you have only sunny days (lucky you!), transplant late in the afternoon. Once you've prepared the growing area (see Chapter 4), dig a large hole for each pot or pellet at the suggested plant spacings. Remember, they will grow much bigger! I use a trowel, digging about 6 inches down and about 4 inches around and loosening the soil in the hole. Dip each pot or pellet into a bucket of water, set each down in its hole, and keep the plants at about the same soil level they were in their pots. (Tomatoes can be set deeper than that into the ground.) Water your newly planted seedlings well, and provide some shelter for a few days. I use a lawn chair, placed over the plants, to provide shade and protection in case of a heavy rain.

Transplant on a cloudy day.

Look at your garden every day, and tell your plants how nice they look. You'll be much more pleased with your results if you get really involved with your garden. And it's so much fun to watch it grow and develop!

Frost

It can be maddening when seed packet directions say "after spring frost is past" or "about a week before the last spring frost." What is frost and why is it important to know about?

When moisture in the air freezes on plant leaves, there is frost. If it's cold enough to freeze the moisture inside the leaves, it is hard frost—which kills tender plants like tomatoes and impatiens. When you are growing such seeds as tomatoes and impatiens, remember these plants are "tender" and unable to live at air temperatures lower than 32 degrees F—even for an hour. Therefore you must know your area's frost dates so you don't put your seedlings out too early. The U.S. Department of Agriculture publishes a detailed map showing "hardiness zones" all over the country. A "hardiness zone" is determined by an area's average lowest winter temperature, the average date of first frost in fall, the average date of last frost in spring, and the average number of growing days in that zone. The County Extension Service can give you this approximate date in your area. Look it up under "County" in your telephone book.

Notes

Chapter 6
Things to Watch For

*W*ill there be a "serpent" in your garden of seedlings? I sure hope not! But this book would be incomplete without a description of things to watch for. They are listed in order of likelihood, so you won't worry needlessly.

By now you can see that seeds are easy to grow. But because we are dealing with living things, in a world of other living things and unpredictable events (including weather), you may experience some problems. I hope this chapter will not discourage you. Remember that nature has been successfully planting seeds for thousands of years, with no help from us, and will continue to do so. It is a method of "plant a lot more than needed" to allow for those situations that may come along. I strongly advise you to do as nature does.

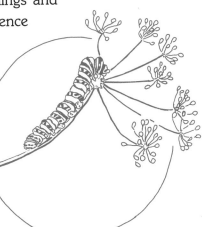

This beautiful green and black caterpillar, sometimes called a parsley worm, is the immature Monarch butterfly. I wouldn't consider one of these as a pest.

Growing Seeds!

What are the primary things to watch for when growing seedlings? This may sound as if I'm joking, but really, avoid the extremes! Here's what I mean. Steady growth is your ideal and the seedling's ideal, too. When temperatures are at an even medium, without huge fluctuations, seedlings have the best environment for steady growth. When soil moisture remains even and constant, the seedling has the unlimited supply of water it requires. When light is maximized during the day and dark prevails at night, as in the natural world, seedlings have the best conditions for growth and rest. When you, as a grower of seeds and plant manager, provide the best environment, you will automatically limit (or even exclude) some problems.

Sometimes, though, you may have a problem with your seeds. Below is a list of problems you may encounter, in order of likelihood. Included is a "hope ratio" to help you evaluate the recovery possibilities for that situation. A 100 percent hope ratio means "not worrisome." (Go have some ice cream instead of worrying.)

Lin's Hope Ratio	Action to Take
0%	Oops! Start over.
50%	Quickly take suggested advice.*
75%	Quickly take suggested advice.*
100%	Do nothing!

*See Table 4 in the appendix for a quick seedling diagnosis, pages 72–73.

What to Look For

Seedlings Tall and Weak

This is probably the most asked seedling question I hear. Tall, weak growth is usually found in seedlings grown indoors, but it sometimes happens outdoors, too. The reason for their spindly condition is that they are stretching for more light. Indoors, they will be leaning toward the nearest light source. Recovery is more likely if you notice this stretching immediately. *Hope ratio:* 75–100 percent.

If indoors, place the seedlings 6 to 8 inches beneath fluorescent lights for 12 to 18 hours a day. (See Chapter 5 for more information.) If outdoors, your seedlings are too crowded together. They must be thinned out so that each plant has space to grow and develop. Thin them when they have just two or three pairs of leaves. If you wait too long to thin them, it may affect their future growth.

Seedlings Pale

This occurs in seedlings grown indoors. If the young seedlings are very young, they are telling you they need more light—in fact they *must* have more light immediately. *Hope ratio:* 75–100 percent.

Luckily, you can do this easily. Place the seedlings 6 to 8 inches beneath fluorescent lights for 12 to 18 hours a day. (See Chapter 5 for more information.) If the seedlings are 6 to 8 weeks old, they need a weak liquid fertilizer solution. (See Chapter 5.)

Lack of Emergence

You have planted the seeds, and according to the seed packet, they're supposed to germinate in 7 to 21 days. You're getting to the end of that period, and no seedlings are showing. With indoor plantings, if the seed-starting mixture is not sterile, if the soil temperatures are consistently low, or if the soil mixture is very wet (or any combination of the above), a fungus called "damping off" may have caused your seeds to rot before they could germinate. Another possibility is that you planted the seeds too deeply. Many need light to germinate. If they are covered too deeply, they cannot emerge. *Hope ratio:* 0–75 percent.

Take a look. If the seeds look unhealthy, moldy, or are missing entirely, start again with a fresh sterile soil mixture. (See Chapter 5.)

With outdoor plantings, look at the soil covering the seeds. If it appears disturbed, birds or squirrels may have found your seeds and dined on them. This is particularly true of sweet corn and sunflower seeds. *Hope ratio:* 0–75 percent.

Plant more seeds immediately. Erect a scarecrow made of aluminum pie tins on string to frighten the critters away. Or, let the kids help you make a real scarecrow. They'll enjoy it. Make sure, though, if you do use a scarecrow, that you change its look and position frequently because birds are smart.

Seedlings Fallen Over

Indoors or outdoors, if your seedlings have keeled over at the soil line and the stem looks pinched there, it is damping off. This fungus does its work underground, or just at the soil level, usually when conditions are cool and wet. Unfortunately they won't revive. *Hope ratio:* 0 percent.

If indoors, start again with a fresh sterile soil mixture. (See Chapter 5.) If outdoors, replant immediately, preferably in a slightly different place. (See Chapter 4.)

Seedlings Cut Off

They were beautiful last evening when you looked at them, but this morning they're cut off and maybe some are even lying around ruined. It's heartbreaking! Your bad guy is either cutworms, who love to work at night, or rabbits, who munch in the early morning. You must replant. *Hope ratio:* 0 percent. *Anger ratio:* 100 percent.

Cutworms frequently cut off tomato, pepper, and eggplant seedlings. To prevent cutworm damage, when you transplant tomato, pepper, or eggplant seedlings, set a plastic or paper cup (with the bottom removed) around the base of each plant, pushing it slightly down into the soil around the stem. Leave it there until the plants are fairly large.

To prevent rabbit damage, well … you can try! Stretch chicken wire or hardware cloth in a tunnel shape over the rows of young salad crops and beans. You can also try regular sprinklings of dried blood (available at garden centers and hardware stores) around the plants (reapply after each rain). I always plant more than I want in case I lose some to the local wildlife.

Leaves Yellowing

If just the bottom leaves are yellow, not to worry. Bottom leaves normally age first and drop off. *Hope ratio:* 75–100 percent.

If your seedlings have been indoors for 6 to 8 weeks, they'll be okay as soon as you get them outside. Transplant them to the garden as soon as possible, watering with a weak fertilizer solution.

If outdoors, sometimes lower leaves are shaded by other plants if their spacing is too close. This may cause lower leaves to yellow and drop off. Also, dry conditions cause lower leaves to yellow. Try to maintain even soil moisture with regular watering, and provide a side-dressing of fertilizer. (See Chapter 5.)

Holes in Leaves

Various larvae (the worm stage of many insects) feed on plant leaves. Beetles (adult stage of insect) can also chew holes in leaves. Usually they don't eat that much, with the exception of the tomato hornworm, a cool-looking, huge green larva that eats a lot. Japanese beetles can also eat a lot, but they usually prefer roses and ornamental plants rather than seedlings. *Hope ratio:* 75–100 percent.

Just pick the critters off and squish 'em, or leave them somewhere the birds can find them.

Seedlings Gone

Outdoors, rabbits and cats can quickly destroy seedlings by eating or digging them up. *Hope ratio:* 0 percent. *Anger ratio:* 100 percent.

As a preventive measure, plant more than you really want. After the fact, replant immediately. Do not kill the cat. Try repellents for pets or dried blood sprinkled around the plants. Reapply it until the plants are large enough to laugh at a rabbit or cat.

Seedlings Withered and Collapsed

You went away and forgot to get a seedling sitter for your indoor "babies"? Your seedlings became completely dried out. *Hope ratio:* 0 percent. *Shame ratio:* 100 percent.

Once they've wilted and collapsed, they won't revive. Live and learn.

Seedlings Suddenly Collapsed

You just put your lovely seedlings out in the sunny garden this morning. Now they're collapsed! They have been badly sunburned and/or windburned, because they were not hardened off. If you discover this just as they are wilting down, cover the plants immediately with shade and water them profusely. They may revive. Otherwise? *Hope ratio:* 0 percent.

To prevent this catastrophe entirely, see Chapter 4.

Sudden Death

This can happen outdoors if there is a strong concentration of granular fertilizer in the planting

soil when you transplant your seedlings to the garden, or when you apply granular fertilizer around plants and it gets on the stems and leaves. Another possibility is that someone sprayed weed killer in the vicinity, and the spray drifted onto your plants. *Hope ratio:* 0 percent. *Anguish ratio:* 100 percent.

Replant. Live and learn.

Honest Advice

Writing about these diseases, insects, and other catastrophes was certainly depressing, so I know reading it was, too. But don't expect these disasters. Just keep an eye out. You may encounter one or two of these problems every year, or just once in a while.

If you do have one of these situations, record it in your journal and don't let it discourage you. Instead, let it teach you. And just take it in stride as a gardener, who always expects the best, is prepared for the worst, and is delighted with what actually grows.

Chapter 7

Keeping Seeds

Gardeners are thrifty and practical. Most hate to throw anything away. Are you that way, too?

I never have any seeds left over because I plant them all, using nature's philosophy. But if you do, and you can't bear to throw them away, here are some suggestions for storing them.

Keep seeds dry when you store them.

Storing Seeds

If you want to keep seeds you haven't used, and want to make sure they stay viable, keep them dry and cool. "Dry" means sealed from moisture, so that neither rain, water, nor humidity can come into contact with them. If moisture is present around seeds, they naturally begin to absorb it. They may swell up with water, or grow mold, in their attempt to germinate. Both of these situations are destructive to a seed. "Cool" means away from sunlight, heat registers, places that heat up or cool down drastically, and areas subject to freezing temperatures.

Growing Seeds!

In the seed business, many companies use a "dry room" for the storage of more sensitive seeds (those with short viability, or very expensive seeds such as hybrid peppers). In a dry room, humidity and temperature are carefully controlled. The percentage of humidity in the room's air, added to the temperature of the air in the dry room, must not exceed 100 percent.

Some seeds are specially packaged in a moisture vapor-locked, plastic film–lined packet. This provides protection for the seeds before they are purchased in the retail store or while they are being shipped. Once a packet like this has been opened, all benefits of the vapor lock are lost.

This should give you an idea of the necessity for cool, dry conditions in the life of a seed being stored for later use.

Keep your unplanted seeds in a dry glass jar with a tight-fitting lid. Put some desiccant inside (such as the little packets often included in shoe boxes that contain silica gel) to absorb any humidity inside the jar. Put the jar in a cool place, and plant the stored seeds as soon as possible.

When you plant seeds, you expect successful germination. Some folks say they expect every seed to germinate, period. If this is the kind of performance you require, try starting with high-viability seed. These are seeds from the current year's seed display, or from a mail-order seed company's current inventory. Most of the time, the seed packet is stamped "Packed for

Leftover Seeds

I've discovered something else about seeds: People cannot throw them away! In a seed packet, say there are one hundred seeds. The cost of a seed packet is very low (less than $2). Take that cost and divide it by the number of seeds, and you will see that, normally, each seed is of low value economically. In fact, it is the least expensive part of gardening. Yet most folks I have spoken with over the years have a special attitude toward the seeds they buy. When people plant seeds and have a few left over afterward, what do they do with them? Throw them away? Never! People keep the seeds they haven't used—in a drawer, in the garden shed or garage—indefinitely. The next time they need seeds, perhaps after a year or two (or even longer), many people plant these leftover seeds or continue to keep them. Why? I believe it's because people consider seeds to be precious. They have an instinctive feeling of their value and potential. And it is true that seeds are precious. They are uniquely and wonderfully made.

(year)." Sometimes you'll get a seed packet that has been overstickered. If you peel this back, you may see that the seed was packed for the previous year. This is okay. What it really means is that, although the seeds were put in the packet the previous year, the seed lot they came from has very recently been tested for germination viability. This germination standard is set by the U.S. government, and the percentage varies depending on the kind of seed in the packet. These seeds, regardless of the date under the sticker, are still fresh, vigorous, viable, and saleable. They will germinate well. Seed companies have special storage capacities that make them successful at holding seeds under the best conditions. Therefore, buy new, fresh seed every year that you know is going to grow for you.

Checking for Germination Before You Plant

Checking for germination is easy to do with medium to large seeds. With small seeds, it's hardly worth the effort, so just plant them. To do a germination test, spread out two or three thick paper towels. Sprinkle well to dampen them. Mix up the seeds well. Take a representative sample of the seeds you want to test (say, ten out of one hundred seeds) and lay them out at equal intervals over the towel. Place another two or three thick paper towels over the seeds. Sprinkle well until all the towels are

Simple germination tests in the kitchen can save a lot of headaches in the garden.

moist, *not wet*. Carefully roll it all up snugly, secure with rubber bands, and slide it inside a clear plastic bag. Leave it on the kitchen counter. Make sure the towels stay moist, not wet. At the end of the suggested germination period, unroll and count the seeds that have germinated. If eight of the ten have sprouted, you have 80 percent germination. You can reroll them and wait a few more days, then check again. A few more may have germinated.

Germination tests are regularly conducted on all lots of seed that a seed company plans to sell. The seed samples are taken in units of a hundred (to provide a large enough sample for reliable results). More than one test is done on one lot (called a replicated test) for the most fair and impartial record of the lot's true viability. Ideal temperature conditions are provided during the testing in special germinator cabinets, which are like refrigerators except that they can be regulated specifically for temperature and light. U.S. government regulations require all flower seed lots to be tested at 6-month intervals, and vegetables at 4-month intervals. The acceptable germination percentages for each type of seed are published, consulted, and strictly adhered to—another reason why you should have confidence in a seed!

Collecting Seeds

You may want to collect your own seeds at some point in your gardening experience—say, from your marigolds, or from a tomato you especially liked, or from meadow flowers in your area. One caution: Do *not* collect seeds from protected plants.

There are two kinds of these: (1) Protected native plants might be found on an endangered list. If you want seeds of these plants, they can be found through specialty catalog seed companies that propagate the seeds in nurseries (thus not threatening the natural reproductive cycle of wild-growing plants). (2) Seeds from plants designated "PVP." This means "Plant Variety Protection," a designation that is similar to a patent. The plant breeder has found something unique (as a part of his or her intellectual property), which he or she wishes to protect. These varieties are so designated on the seed packet or on the plant stake when you purchase them.

Cover the maturing flower with a paper bag.

"Everything has a season" and that is just as true of a seed as it is of a tomato. The tricky part is that, while it's easy to tell when a tomato is ripe, it's not so easy to tell with a seed. Ripeness is important if you want to collect seeds, because if you collect them before they are ripe, they will probably not germinate (they're not "done" yet). If you try to collect them after they are ripe, they may already be gone (dehisced or dispersed), because ripening can happen quickly. A seed collector must be very observant and patient with the process and its timing. You will learn a lot during your first collecting experience.

Meadow plants: Wait until several flowers are starting to fade, then slip a paper bag upside down over each flower. Fasten it tightly around (but don't choke) the stem. Check it daily until you hear seeds skittering around in the bag. Cut the flower stalk off, turn the bag right side up, and shake the flower stalk inside the bag until the seeds have all been shed into the bag. If they won't come off, they're not quite ripe. Try again in a week or so. When you've harvested your seeds, make sure they are completely dry. Package them in an envelope or baby food jar, label them, and store them as described on page 47.

Marigolds and other flowers: Follow the same procedure already described. You can clip the fading flower heads into a large paper bag as they begin to dry, then follow the previous suggestions.

Beans, peas, corn (dry seeds): Let the chosen pods or ears stay on the plant until completely dry, but cut them off and put them in a paper bag before the pods split open and disperse the seeds, or before the birds, squirrels, or raccoons get to them.

Tomatoes, cucumbers, other fruits and vegetables with seeds in their flesh (wet seeds): Getting seeds from these can be a little smelly! Select the fruit you want (the biggest, the reddest, or whatever your criteria are) and set it somewhere undisturbed until it starts to go bad and gooey (when seeds are fully ripe). Then squeeze out the juice and seeds, or cut open the fruit and scrape the seeds into a jar. Add water. Let the jar sit at room temperature for 24 hours. Hold your nose! Rinse the seeds in running water by pouring the mess through a sieve. If the flesh is still adhering, repeat for another day or several days. Spread the wet, cleaned seeds out on a wire screen and let them dry thoroughly for several days or more. *They must be thoroughly dry.*

While they're drying, protect them from rodents, who seem to know when you're drying something yummy. Then package and label your seeds, and store them in a cool, dry place.

Saved Seed and Diversity

When you save seeds from flowering or fruiting plants, you may notice a difference—from small to great—in the results you receive from subsequent plantings. The flowers may differ in color or shape from the flowers you collected them from. The fruits may be different in flavor, color, or maturity. The plants may even have a different habit.

This diversity is considered a good thing by plant breeders and environmentalists, but it can be disappointing to a home gardener. Diversity is due to plant genetics, which I explain in the next chapter.

Notes

Chapter 8

Where Seeds Come From

Where do seedless watermelon seeds come from?

One could say that seeds come from plants, and plants come from seeds. True—but this would make you crazy, and there's so much more to say! This question is a good one, and leads to a discussion of the structure and purpose of flowers.

Almost all plants have flowers. That sounds so obvious—we know marigolds have flowers, and cucumber plants have flowers, but have you ever seen a cabbage flower? How about a maple tree? A pine tree? A carrot? They *all* have flowers.

Why are there flowers? It is the way that plants reproduce. Flowers are the reproductive organs of plants. The flower's only purpose is to produce seeds within itself so it can grow again next year. Simple! Complicated!

Growing Seeds!

Simple Plant Genetics

Plants make their seeds with genetic programs that ensure offspring like them. Seeds are produced by processes that take place through special flower parts inside the flower. All flowers have several parts, but not all flowers have the same parts or even the same number of parts.

We love flowers for their beauty, but all we normally notice are the flower petals—the showy parts. So let's look at the other parts, too. Starting at the flower stem, first is the calyx, to which the rest of the parts are attached. There are green leaflike parts on the outside, called sepals. The petals are next—and there may be just a few, or hundreds. Then, in the center of the flower, we find the stigma, style, and ovary (female parts), and the stamen and anthers (male parts). These parts come in all sizes, too. Even a very tiny flower has many parts, which we don't even think about.

Botanically, a flower with all these parts is called a "perfect" flower. Even if it looks kind of raggedy to us, it's still perfect when it contains all these structures. A perfect flower has all it needs to self-pollinate (transfer its pollen from the pollen sacs to the stigma), although help is often required in the form of wind or insects. When a breeze blows over the flower, it loosens ripe pollen grains and makes them soar over to the sticky stigma and land there. The pollen grains then "grow" down through the style to the

Pollen grain
Stigma
Pollen tube
Style
Ovary
Anther and pollen
Stamen
Petal
Sepal
Developing ovule

Cross section of a flower showing parts and the process of pollination.

ovary. Pollination is now complete, and seeds developing in the ovary will be the result. Many flowers are specifically designed to attract insects that help the pollen transfer among the flower parts. Petal markings and fragrance are two ways a flower attracts insects. When a flower receives pollen from structures within itself, its genetic makeup is predictable and known. When pollen from one flower is brought to a different flower, it brings different genetic possibilities with it. The more sources for pollen there are, the greater the possibility of different combinations of genes. This is also known as genetic diversity.

Now, suppose we look at a flower and find only the stigma, style, and ovary inside the petals. This flower is "imperfect." An imperfect flower is one that has either female or male parts, but not both. Since a flower's sole purpose is to make seeds, where will the pollen come from? In this case, the "female" flower must receive pollen from another flower because it has none itself. Without this transfer of pollen, the flower will dry up without producing seeds. Nature wants to prevent this. So this flower relies on cross-pollination. Wind, an insect, or an animal helps the flower receive pollen. Squash and cucumbers are examples of plants with imperfect flowers: They produce separate male and female flowers on the same plant.

So, What Is a Hybrid?

Today when we talk about hybrids in the seed business, we refer mostly to a plant that is the result of a process of pollination and harvesting controlled by human decision and action. Many seeds offered for sale today are "hybrids." It's good for a gardener to understand what makes a certain variety hybrid and why the seed of a hybrid variety is usually more expensive.

Let's take a well-known hybrid as an example: the Big Boy tomato. When you buy Big Boy hybrid tomato seed, it always grows into the expected Big Boy tomato plant, which bears (finally, at the end of the summer) Big Boy tomatoes. This is a certainty. What goes into making the seed of the Big Boy hybrid tomato? (It is described as "making" because it is purposefully planned and executed.) This popular tomato was one of the earliest hybrids developed for home gardening.

In the 1940s, plant breeders observed some interesting tomato plants among a whole lot of other tomato plants they had grown in what are called "trials"—seeds from various controlled pollinations are grown out as hybrid plants and carefully observed by specialists.

These breeders looked back at their records to determine which plants they had used in the pollination process that produced these interesting tomato plants. "Plant X" had been known to produce a very flavorful tomato. "Plant Y" was seen to grow big tomatoes. So, as part of a plan to develop a tomato with both of these characteristics, plant breeders took tomato pollen (male part) from Plant X and applied

it by hand to the tomato flowers on Plant Y (female part). Then they covered the pollinated flower on Plant Y with a bag to exclude all other pollen. The fruit that developed from the polli- nated flower contained the seeds that grew into the interesting tomato plants, later dubbed "Big Boy." These seeds contained a predictable genetic heri- tage from both Plant X and Plant Y.

So, a hybrid is the result of a controlled cross of two selected parent plants in order to pro- duce a specific combination of traits of both par- ent plants into one plant.

I hope this makes sense, because the real kicker is that, once an interesting plant has been grown from a controlled cross between two selected plants, it has to be re-created by the same controlled cross every year, using the same parent plants X and Y, by hand-pollination of tiny tomato flowers, bagging, careful harvesting, drying, and pack- aging, to make sure that every time you buy a package of Big Boy hybrid tomato seeds, it will be the *same* great tomato you grew last year, and the year before, and the year before that.

To get back to the opening question of this chapter, "Where do seedless watermelon seeds come from?" you can now see that they are produced in, and harvested from, the developed ovary of female flowers of a selected watermelon plant, which was pollinated by hand with the pollen of a selected male parent plant. In addition, in the case

Have you ever wondered where seeds come from?

Growing Seeds!

of the formation of seedless (or "triploid") watermelons, one of the parent plants has been altered by an application of colchicine, a plant extract, to change its chromosome count.

Therefore, these hybrid seeds, harvested from the watermelon just described, have special extra chromosomes, which make their off-spring sterile (unable to produce seeds). When you plant them, the fruit they produce has no (or sometimes a few soft) seeds in it. This makes a tasty treat for us—but for the propagation of a future generation, human intervention is again required in order to cross-pollinate, grow, and harvest seeds from the same parent watermelon plants year after year.

Hybrid seeds cost more than open-pollinated (naturally pollinated) seeds, because they require planning, hand labor, and very careful attention to detail. However, when you grow a hybrid you like, you'll find the extra seed cost well worth it. And in the case of seedless watermelon, only a hybrid will do!

Chapter 9
Other Stuff

About Mother Nature ...

No matter what seeds you grow, you'll enjoy the adventure. It is always an adventure, because climate is the one aspect of growing seeds that we can neither predict nor control. This may drive you crazy; but on the other hand, it's an interesting variable that makes each year's garden slightly different, and often provides a wonderful surprise or two. You'll discover plants that reseed themselves year after year in your garden, and this is really interesting! I encourage you to keep a journal about your seed-growing experiences. It will be fun to look at, year after year. Write down the weather conditions that nature presented you with. This information will become a treasure, too, as you record your garden experiences with seeds!

Some Handy Tips

About Carrots

Carrot seed takes a little while to germinate. Heavy rains that fall after planting can cause the soil to get packed down. So mix some radish seed in with your carrot seed when you plant. The radish seed will germinate fast, breaking up the hard soil, letting the moisture in, and allowing the seedlings to come up. Keep the top of the soil moist so a hard crust does not form, until the carrots germinate.

About Morning Glories

About 2 hours before you go out to plant your morning glory seeds, put them in a glass jar and soak them in room-temperature water. Do not soak longer than 12 hours or their oxygen supply will be cut off and they will die. To help a seed imbibe water more quickly when planted, use an emery board to run across each seed just enough to scratch through ("scar" or "scarify") the seed coat without damaging the internal parts of the seed (the white part that shows through, the cotyledon). Provide support for the plants right away—you'll be surprised how quickly they begin to vine.

About Parsley

About 2 hours before you plant your parsley seeds, indoors or out, put them in a glass jar and soak them in room-temperature water. Do not soak them longer than 12 hours.

Germinating Seeds Fast Indoors

Plant your seeds, then cover the pot or flat with a clear plastic bag. Place it on top of the refrigerator (or the TV, if it is on all day) and check it every day for signs of green. The bottom heat helps the seeds imbibe water and begin their emergence. As soon as the first seedling appears, put the pot or flat under lights (see Chapter 5). This procedure gives you a lot of satisfaction, and the warmth can prevent some seedling diseases, too. It works especially well for impatiens, pepper, and eggplant.

Planting BIG Seeds

A good rule to remember is that seeds should be planted about one and a half to two times as deep as they are big. A lima bean seed about $1/2$ inch long, then, should be covered by about $1 1/2$ inches of soil. For quicker germination, soak them as described for morning glories. Many people have inquired over the years, "Does it matter which side is up when I plant my beans?" The bean seed has a very noticeable "belly button" (called the hilum), which is the place where the radicle will emerge. If you want to be very disciplined about planting your bean seeds, you can make sure that the "belly button" is pointing downward. But don't worry if you don't do this! Both the radicle and the shoot will know which way to grow, and will grow in the right direction.

Planting EARLY Outdoors in Spring

You can get quicker, surer germination of early-planted seeds, such as those of peas, pansies, sweet peas, or spinach, by warming up the soil before you plant. If the soil is dry enough to stir up, do so, and then stretch black plastic film over it. Anchor the plastic and wait about a week. Then plant your seeds right through the plastic (use a penknife or dibble to make the holes). Seeds such as lettuce don't need this treatment. Just plant them in prepared soil and press in (don't cover; lettuce needs light to germinate).

Planting Tiny Seeds

Some seeds, such as those of petunias, impatiens, and snapdragons, are so tiny they look like dust. These tiny seeds often cost a little more, too, so you want to get the best results you can. Tiny seeds are usually best started indoors so you can keep an eye on them. Prepare your pots or flats first. Then pour the seeds into your palm, shaking the packet carefully to get them all out. Take a pinch of seeds and sprinkle them over each pot. Then water the seeds into the soil with a fine mist. Cover the pots with clear plastic. Bottom heat is good (see "Germinating Seeds Fast Indoors") to get these tiny seeds going quickly. As soon as you see green, put the pots under lights.

Watering Seedlings

When you apply a stream of water to small seedlings, it may wash them to one side or even knock them over. Either water from above with a mister, applying enough to soak down into the soil as far as the roots, or set the pot into a tray with an inch or two of water, and let it sit there until the pot has soaked up enough water from the tray to make the soil surface dark (usually 1 to 2 hours). This is the most certain way of wetting the entire soil mass.

Appendix

Tables

Table 1
Seed Growing Guidelines

SIMPLE	EASY	CAN BE TRICKY	CHALLENGING	MOST CHALLENGING
Bean	Annual Baby's Breath	Broccoli	Belgian Endive	Helianthemum
Marigold	Basil	Bulb Onions	(Chicon)	Rosemary
Radish	Beet	Cabbage	Brussels Sprout	Tree Seed
Sunflower	Black-Eyed Susan	California Poppy	Lavender	Woody Shrub
Zinnia	Bunching Onion	Canna	Tritoma	Woody Vine
	Candytuft	Canterbury Bell		
	Cantaloupe	Carnation		
	Cardinal Climber	Carrot		
	Celosia	Castor Bean		
	Chinese Lantern	Cauliflower		
	Chive	Chrysanthemum		
	Cleome	Corn*		
	Collard	Delphinium		
	Cosmos	Eggplant		
	Cucumber	Endive		
	Dahlia	Flower Mixture*		
	Echinacea	Foxglove		
	Forget-Me-Not	Hibiscus		
	Four O'Clock	Hollyhock		
	Gaillardia	Iceland Poppy		
	Globe Amaranth	Impatiens		
	Gourd	Larkspur		
	Hesperis	Leek		
	Kale	Moonflower		
	Kochia	Nicotiana		
	Kohlrabi	Oriental Poppy		

SIMPLE	EASY	CAN BE TRICKY	CHALLENGING	MOST CHALLENGING
	Lavatera	Ornamental Grass		
	Lettuce	Pansy		
	Liatris	Parsley		
	Linum	Pea		
	Lunaria	Peanut		
	Lupine	Pepper		
	Morning Glory	Perennial Gypsophila		
	Moss Rose	Petunia		
	Nasturtium	Salvia		
	Nigella	Snapdragon		
	Painted Daisy	Stock		
	Phlox	Sweet Pea		
	Pumpkin	Verbena		
	Roquette	Vinca		
	Shasta Daisy	Viola		
	Spinach	Wallflower		
	Squash	Watermelon		
	Strawflower			
	Sweet William			
	Swiss Chard			
	Tithonia			
	Tomato			
	Turnip			

Table 2
Lin's Recipe for Seed-Starting Mixture

INGREDIENTS	QUANTITIES	DIRECTIONS	STORING
Peat Moss	Equal quantities (about 2 cups) of each	Keep proportional no matter how much you mix up	I keep mixture in a bucket indoors. It stores well indefinitely.
Top Soil, sterile	Equal quantities (about 2 cups) of each	If there are any large lumps, break up. Mix everything together with your hands.	Also fine for repotting houseplants and growing plants in large containers outdoors.
Perlite and/or Vermiculite	Equal quantities (about 2 cups) of each	Add a cup or so of water, stir up to moisten. Add more water if you're mixing a lot.	Sift loosely into peat pots for seed storing. Do not pack.

Table 3: Timing

For Starting Seeds Indoors: Spring Crop

Zone	Suggested Timing for Spring and Summer Harvest or Bloom	Tomato*	Pepper*	Eggplant*	Onion*
Zone 3 Zone 3	Start Indoors Transplant Outdoors	April 10 June 1	March 30 June 1	March 15 June 1	Feb. April
Zone 4 Zone 4	Start Indoors Transplant Outdoors	April 10 June 1	March 30 June 1	March 15 June 1	Feb. April
Zone 5 Zone 5	Start Indoors Transplant Outdoors	April 10 June 1	March 30 June 1	March 15 June 1	Jan.–Feb. March–April
Zone 6 Zone 6	Start Indoors Transplant Outdoors	March–April May–June	March–April May–June	March May–June	Jan.–Feb. March–April
Zone 7 Zone 7	Start Indoors Transplant Outdoors	March–April May–June	March May–June	March May–June	Dec.–Jan. Feb.–April
Zone 8 Zone 8	Start Indoors Transplant Outdoors	Feb. 1 March–May	Jan. Feb.–April	Feb.–March March–April	Dec.–Jan. Dec.–Jan.
Zones 9 & 10 Zones 9 & 10	Start Indoors Transplant Outdoors	Feb. 1 March–May	Dec.–Jan. Feb.–March	Oct.–Nov. Dec.–March	Dec.–Jan. Dec.–Jan.

*Outdoor planting time for these items is after the spring frost.

Table 3 (cont.): Timing
For Starting Seeds Indoors: Spring Crop

Zone	Suggested Timing for Spring and Summer Harvest or Bloom	Impatiens*	Petunia*	Vinca*	Geranium, Verbena*
Zone 3 Zone 3	Start Indoors Transplant Outdoors	March June 1	March 15 June 1	Feb. 20 June 1	Feb. 15 June 1
Zone 4 Zone 4	Start Indoors Transplant Outdoors	March June 1	March 15 June 1	March 1 June 1	Feb. 15 June 1
Zone 5 Zone 5	Start Indoors Transplant Outdoors	March June 1	March 15 June 1	March 15 June 1	Feb. 15 June 1
Zone 6 Zone 6	Start Indoors Transplant Outdoors	March 15 late May	March late May	Feb. late May	Jan. late May
Zone 7 Zone 7	Start Indoors Transplant Outdoors	Mar–Apr Apr–May	Feb.–March April–May	Feb.–March April–May	Jan.–Feb. April–May
Zone 8 Zone 8	Start Indoors Transplant Outdoors	Dec.–Jan. Feb.–May	Feb.–March March–May	Feb. March–June	Feb. March–May
Zones 9 & 10 Zones 9 & 10	Dec.–Jan. Dec.–Jan.	Jan.–Feb. Feb.–May	July–Jan. Sept.–March	Jan.–April March–July	July–Jan. Sept.–March

* Outdoor planting time for these items is after the spring frost.

Table 3 (cont.): Timing
For Starting Seeds Outdoors: Summer Crop

Zone	Suggested Timing for Fall and Winter Harvest or Bloom	Crop			
		Broccoli Brussels Sprouts (6–8 weeks)	Cabbage Cauliflower (6 weeks)	Pansy, Other Hardy Annuals	Perennial & Biennial Flower Seeds
Zone 3 Start Indoors		March–May	April–May	May–June	May–June
Zone 3 Transplant Outdoors		May–June	May–June	May–June	May–June
Zone 4 Start Indoors		Feb.–March	Feb.–March	May–June	May–June
Zone 4 Transplant Outdoors		April–June	April–May	May–June	May–June
Zone 5 Start Indoors		Feb.–March May–June	Feb.–March May–June	April–May	April–May
Zone 5 Transplant Outdoors		March–April	March–April June–July	June–Aug. June–July	June–Aug.
Zone 6 Start Indoors		June 1	June 1	x	x
Zone 6 Transplant Outdoors		Aug. 1	Aug. 1	June–Aug.	June–Aug.
Zone 7 Start Indoors		Feb–March July–Aug.	Feb–Mar July–Aug.	x	x
Zone 7 Transplant Outdoors		March–April July–Aug.	March–April July–Aug.	June–Aug.	June–Aug.
Zone 8 Start Indoors		Feb.–March July–Aug.	Feb.–March July–Aug.	x	x
Zone 8 Transplant Outdoors		March–April Aug.–Oct.	March–April Aug.–Oct.	June–Aug.	June–Aug.
Zones 9 &10 Start Indoors		x	x	x	x
Zones 9 &10 Plant Outdoors		Broccoli July–Dec. B. Sprouts April–June	Cabbage Sep.–Feb. Cauliflower June–Oct.	Aug.–Dec.	x

Table 4
Diagnosing Seedling Conditions

Description of Your Seedlings	Where Occurring	Hope Ratio	Probable Cause	Suggestions
Seedlings Pale?	Indoors	50–75%	Need more light; too wet	Provide brighter light 12–18 hours/day; add less water or water lightly more frequently; water more frequently.
Seedlings Tall and Weak?	Indoors	50–75%	Need more light; air temperature too high	Brighter light 12–18 hours/day; lower air temperature, especially at night.
Seedlings Tall and Weak?	Outdoors		Plants too crowded together	Thin plants to spacings suggested on seed packet.
Did Not Germinate?	Indoors	0–75%	Seeds planted too deeply; damping off	Replant right away, using fresh seed-starting mixture.
Did Not Germinate?	Outdoors		Seeds planted too deeply; damping off; birds; squirrels	Replant to depth suggested on seed packet or even more shallowly; replant a little later when soil is warmer. Birds or squirrels may have dug up and eaten the seed so you'll have to replant (especially sweet corn, peanuts and sunflower seed).
Seedlings Fallen Over?	Indoors	0%	Damping off	Replant right away, using fresh seed-starting mixture.
Seedlings Fallen Over?	Outdoors	0–50%	Windburn; planted too shallowly	Provide shade if this happens right after you transplanted; in case of the wind, plants will usually straighten up by themselves. Check to see that seedlings are well anchored in soil.
Seedlings Suddenly Cut Off?	Outdoors	0%	Cutworms; rabbits; mate with mower	Cutworms strike at night (esp. tomato transplants); put collar around when setting out. Replant ones the cutworms got. Rabbits likely to eat the plants on the edges of the garden; plant more than you need. Mate with mower? Sorry, no suggestions.

Description of Your Seedlings	Where Occurring	Hope Ratio	Probable Cause	Suggestions
Leaves Yellowing?	Indoors	75–100%	Need to be outdoors in garden; need nutrients	Bottom leaves usually age first and drop off. Transplant to the garden as soon as possible, watering with a weak fertilizer solution.
Leaves Yellowing?	Outdoors		Leaves at bottom?	Lower leaves shaded by other plants (not spaced widely enough). Dry soil may cause lower leaves to yellow. Maintain even soil moisture; side-dress or use fertilizer solution. Top leaves: feed plants with fertilizer solution.
Holes in Leaves?	Outdoors	100%	Unidentified chewing critter	Various larvae/chewing insects feed on plant leaves. Usually they don't eat that much. Just pick critters off and feed them to the chickens or squash them.
Seedlings Gone?	Outdoors	0%	Rabbits; cats	Rabbits and cats can quickly destroy seedlings. Plant more than you want/replant immediately. Try repellents for pets or dried blood sprinkled around the plants.
Seedlings Withered and Collapsed?	Indoors	0%	Dried out while you were away	Seedlings became completely dried out. Once they've wilted and collapsed, they won't revive. Live and learn. Replant.
Seedlings Suddenly Collapsed?	Outdoors	0-50%	Sunburn, windburn; drying out	Badly sunburned and/or windburned, because they were not hardened off. If you discover this immediately, as they are wilting down, cover plants immediately to shade and water profusely.
Sudden Death?	Wherever	0%	Fertilizer burn, weedkiller	Granular fertilizer burn (too much in soil, or coming in contact with stems/leaves), or drift from weed-killer applied nearby.

Lin's Hope Ratio	Suggested Action to Take
0%	Oops! Start over
50%	Quickly take advice above
75%	Quickly take advice above
100%	Do nothing!

Glossary

Anther—A male flower stalk that bears the pollen sac at its outer end.

Balanced Fertilizer—Balanced means a fertilizer that contains nitrogen, phosphorus, and potassium, the three most important plant nutrients. Balanced fertilizers have three numbers on their label, such as 5-10-5, which refer to the percentage of available nitrogen, phosphorus, and potassium in the formula.

Botany—The science of the study of plants; their classification, identification, processes, uses, and functions.

Broadcast—The practice of casting (or dispensing) on the ground by hand, as seed in sowing; opposed to sowing in drills or rows.

Bud—A dormant shoot on the stem of a plant, which, when stimulated by inner processes, will become a shoot and stem that bear leaves and possibly flowers.

Challenging—I have used this term when referring to certain seeds that need pampering or some sort of extra treatment (or extra patience) to get them started. See Table 1 in the appendix.

Cold Frame—A structure consisting of four sides and a movable top, which, when placed on the soil outside, creates a sheltered growing area. The main benefit of a cold frame is to extend the gardening season, in both spring and fall. Cold-frame growing is the best of both worlds for a seedling.

Growing Seeds!

Cotyledon—"Seed leaves," the special storage leaves already formed inside a seed, which first emerge from a seed and have a seedlike shape. They contain stored food to nourish the seedling until it can form true leaves and begin manufacturing its own food.

County Agent—The County Extension Agent is a trained horticultural professional who works for the government's Agricultural Extension Service. The extension office is listed in the phone book under the name of your county. In rural counties, these folks often are dedicated solely to helping farmers with agricultural concerns, because of the economic importance of their crops. In urban areas, county agents are frequently involved in community gardening and beautification efforts. Often they have a staff of trained volunteers called "Master Gardeners" who are available to answer questions.

Cross-pollination—An important process involving the transfer of pollen from one flower, a "male" flower, to the stigma of another, "female" flower or parent plant. Without pollination, seeds would not be made or formed. Also see *Self-pollination*.

Damping Off—A fungus disease that may develop in cool, wet soil and can attack a seed as it germinates or a seedling after it has emerged from the soil. In the first case, it may prevent seedling emergence in certain pots or flats, or just in one area of the pot. In the second case, damping off will cause seedlings to keel over at the soil line because of a pinched area affected by the fungus.

Dehisced—In botany, to open, such as with seed capsules or pods of plants.

Dibble—A tool used for poking holes of any size in the soil for planting. A dibble can be a pencil stub, the blade of trowel, a special tool with a pointed end, a bulb planter, or your finger. A dibble is used for planting ("setting") small plants securely into the ground.

Dormancy—A state of suspension whereby a viable seed is "sleeping" because it has not finished certain maturing processes, it has not been stimulated by such external circumstances as moisture, cold, or heat that signal it to grow, or it has not yet been planted.

Easy—In reference to seeds, the ones you can literally throw on the garden, walk away, and still get beautiful results—no worry, no maintenance. These seeds, listed in Table 1 in the appendix, are excellent for children, new gardeners, busy gardeners, and elderly gardeners (in other words, just about anybody).

Epicotyl—The part of a seedling that grows above the cotyledons, producing the true leaves and the top growth of a plant.

Fertilizer—A substance containing plant nutrients that is added to soil to make it more fertile (capable of growing plants).

Flat—Also known as pack or pot. A rectangular tray with drainage holes, sometimes with individual cells, for filling with potting mixture and starting seeds.

Flower—A reproductive structure of a plant. It consists of several parts, which are not necessarily present in every one. These are the calyx, sepal, petal, ovary, style, stigma, anther, pollen sac, and pollen grains. Petals are the showy part of the flower.

Foot-candles—A measure of the brightness (intensity) of light. A uniform light source puts out a specified intensity of light. Say, in this case, the light source is a candle. The light of a candle would be of equal brightness 1 foot away from the candle in all directions. If the light source did not move, but the surface on which it shone moved away another foot, the intensity of that light would be much reduced (although it would still be of equal brightness in all directions). See Chapter 5 for details.

Germination—The process by which a seed breaks its sleeping state, imbibes water and oxygen, and begins producing enzymes that help it to unfurl its internal structures (radicle, hypocotyl, epicotyl, and cotyledons) and produce a growing plant.

Growing Medium—The soil chosen to grow seeds indoors. Also known as potting mixture. It usually contains various ingredients such as peat moss, perlite/vermiculite, fertilizer, water, and air.

Harden Off—A process undertaken to gradually accustom an indoor-grown plant to outdoor conditions. Seedlings are exposed in a protected place for longer and longer periods for a week or so before they are planted outdoors.

Hardiness Zone—The United States has many different growing climates. Hardiness zones are established by the USDA, predicting the average lowest winter temperature for each area. It is important to know your hardiness zone when growing trees, shrubs, hedges, woody ornamental plants, and perennial flowers. Your hardiness zone determines which plants you will be able to grow successfully. Your county extension office can tell you what your hardiness zone is.

Horticulture—The culture (growing) of flowers, vegetables, herbs, fruits, or ornamental plants.

Hybrid—A plant that results from seeds produced by the controlled cross-pollination of selected parent plants, in order to establish certain traits from both parents. Hybrids are therefore much more predictable in their behavior and uniform in their performance. A seed company must repeat the same controlled cross-pollination every season in order to harvest the hybrid seeds, adding to the cost of the seed.

Hypocotyl—The part of a seedling that grows below the cotyledon and just above the radicle (primary root). It becomes the base of the stem of the mature plant.

Imperfect Flower—A flower that has either female or male parts, but not both. The female parts of the imperfect flower must receive pollen from the male parts of another imperfect flower in order to be pollinated. Without this transfer of pollen, the flower will dry up without producing seeds.

Leaf—A special food-manufacturing plant structure, within which are found specialized cells called chloroplasts, where sunlight is converted into food energy. Leaves are also a reliable plant signature, since the shape, size, and color of a leaf makes it possible to identify a plant.

Master Gardener—A volunteer who has completed a certain number of hours of training under his or her county's Agricultural Extension Service, and then has spent an equal or greater number of hours of volunteer service helping people in the county with gardening programs or projects.

Mulch—A layer 1–3 inches deep, spread over the ground around plants to control weeds, conserve soil moisture, and keep plant roots cool (or warm).

Materials for mulching include peat moss, compost, shredded bark, grass clippings, shredded licorice root, or layers of newspaper. Black plastic film is an excellent mulch for vegetables.

NPK—Chemical symbols for the elements nitrogen, phosphorus, and potassium, the three most important plant nutrients. The percent of available NPK in a fertilizer is given on the label by three numbers separated with dashes, such as 5-10-5 (5% nitrogen, 10% phosphorus, and 5% potassium). The order of the elements is always the same.

Open-pollinated—A plant that results from seeds, which develop as a result of pollination by wind or bees, occurring in a seed production field. Open-pollinated plants can show a greater range of variables in size, uniformity, and maturity. This trait is valued for permitting genetic diversity.

Ovary—The base of the flower's female structures, where seeds are formed after a flower has been successfully pollinated.

Peat Moss—A basic organic material component in a seed-starting mixture or growing medium. Peat moss is harvested from peat bogs in the northern area of the United States and Canada and compacted into bales for purchase. It can be added to garden soil or used as a mulch.

Perfect Flower—A flower with all the parts required (male and female structures) to self-pollinate and produce seeds.

Perlite—Expanded volcanic rock, white in color, that is a common ingredient in a seed-starting mixture or growing medium. It increases drainage and air circulation and lightens the texture and weight of soil mixtures.

Petals—The outer parts of a flower, usually showy and brightly colored, that surround and protect the inner, central reproductive parts. Petals often have special markings that attract pollinating insects to the flower.

Phloem—Part of the vascular system within a plant, consisting of special tubes for transporting solutes (food) downward to the roots. The vascular system is located along the outside of stem and root.

Photosynthesis—The process by which plants make their own food. Within specialized structures called chloroplasts, sunlight (radiant energy) converts carbon dioxide and hydrogen into carbohydrates using chlorophyll (chemical energy). Chlorophyll is the green pigment in plants.

Pistil—The female structures within a flower.

Pollen—Tiny grains, of characteristic shape, color, and size for each type of plant, that are produced by the male parts of a flower for the purpose of pollinating the female parts of the same or a similar flower, and thereby forming seeds by which the plant can reproduce itself.

Pollination—The process by which pollen from the male parts of flowers is transferred to the female parts of a flower, thus forming seeds.

Pricking Out—Selectively transplanting plants that have been grown indoors to a larger pot or a garden outdoors.

PVP—This designation, Plant Variety Protection, refers to a plant that has a patent status, applied for and granted through the USDA. Such plants are so marked and should not be propagated for profit.

Radicle—The primary root, the first structure to emerge from the planted seed, which then produces the root system.

Scarification—A method to help seeds imbibe water more quickly when planted, used on seeds with a very hard or thick seed coat. I use an emery board to run across each seed just enough to scratch through ("scar" or "scarify") the seed coat without damaging the internal parts of the seed (the white part that shows through, the cotyledon).

Seed—The fertilized, ripened ovule of a seed-producing plant, containing a plant embryo capable of germinating and producing a new plant.

Seed-starting Mix—Also known as growing medium or potting mixture. A soil medium for growing seeds indoors. It contains various ingredients such as peat moss, perlite/vermiculite, fertilizer, water, and air. For starting seeds, this mixture should be sterile or sterilized before using it for planting.

Self-pollination—The process of transferring pollen from the male parts of a flower to the female parts of the same flower. Without pollination, seeds would not be made or formed. Also see *Cross-pollination*.

Sepal—The outer flower petals, usually green and sometimes of a different shape than the inner petals, which protect the flower bud before it opens and often help to support the petals after the flower has unfurled.

Soaking—A method for encouraging medium and large seeds to germinate quickly. Letting seeds sit in lukewarm water for 2 hours or less.

Soil—A substance consisting of granular or powdered rock, organic material, water, air, nutritional chemicals, and organisms, which forms the basis of plant life, growth, and nourishment on earth. Also a mixture made by human hands, containing various ingredients such as garden soil, peat moss, perlite/vermiculite, fertilizer, water, and air.

Solutes—Substances such as sugars, salts, minerals, and chemical compounds, dissolved or carried in water, that are absorbed from the soil or manufactured in the leaves of a plant and carried throughout the plant.

Sowing—The horticultural term for planting, referring only to the activity of planting seeds. One does not sow a tree or a bulb; one sows a seed.

Stem—A plant structure of both strength and conductivity, containing vascular tissues and cells with strong supporting walls, that supports the leaves and flowers.

Stigma—The outer end of the female flower part, which is usually sticky so it can "catch" flying pollen grains. In some flowers the stigma is the source of the fragrance that attracts insects.

Stratifying—A process that introduces a hot period to some types of seeds in order to get them to germinate. With some tree seeds, the extreme heat caused by a forest fire can act as a trigger mechanism for germination. Stratifying actually "fools" the seed into thinking that natural processes are taking place, or have taken place. It can help the internal seed structures to mature to the point of germination, or signal the seed that it is time to break its dormancy and grow.

Thinning—The process of spacing seedlings for their optimum growth, either by cutting off surrounding seedlings or transplanting seedlings into individual pots.

Transplanting—Removing seedlings from their seed-starting container and moving them to a larger pot, moving seedlings from indoors to outdoors, or moving seedlings from one place in the garden to another.

Trials—A regular program of growing flowers and vegetables from seed in plots that are observed, compared, and judged for performance and trueness. Trials are maintained and operated at most seed companies, especially commercial ones.

True Leaves—The first leaves to form above the cotyledons (seed leaves). Different in appearance from the cotyledons, they are tiny copies of the mature plant's leaves and are capable of manufacturing food for the seedling plant.

Vascular—The system that conducts fluids—water and substances in solution (solutes)—from the root tip to the shoot tip of a plant.

Vermiculite—A product made of heat-expanded mica rock, of a silvery gray color, used as an addition to soil either in the garden or in soil mixtures. It increases moisture retention, drainage, and air circulation in the soil or soil mixture.

Viability—The ability of a seed to germinate. It is sometimes referred to as longevity, since viability varies in different types of seeds (peppers, short; beans, long).

Wow!—What you will say when the plants you've grown from seeds have bloomed and produced.

Xylem—Part of the vascular system within a plant, consisting of special tubes that conduct water and nutrients upward to the leaves. The vascular system is located along the outside of stem and root.

Suggested Reading

For more information on starting seeds and gardening, check out these excellent books.

Anderson, Jim, and Susan A. McClure. *Seeds and Propagation* (Smith & Hawken). Workman Publishing Co., 1997.

Bubel, Nancy. The *New Seed Starter's Handbook.* Rodale Press, 1988.

Carter, Louise. *Basic Gardening: A Handbook for Beginning Gardeners.* Fulcrum, 1995.

Damrosch, Barbara; Ray Maher and Carol Bolt, illus. *The Garden Primer.* Workman Publishing Co., 1988.

Loewer, Peter. *Seeds: The Definitive Guide to Growing, History & Lore.* Macmillan, 1995.

Lloyd, Christoper, and Graham Rice. *Garden Flowers from Seed.* Timber Press, 1994.

Growing Seeds!

MacCaskey, Michael, and eds. of the National Gardening Association. *Gardening for Dummies.* IDG Books Worldwide Inc., 1996.

Park Seed Company's *The Park Gardener's Handbook,* various articles and authors, at www.parkseed.com/gdnbook. May 1997.

Polson, Carol. "Containing Your Vegetable Garden." In *Natural Land's* "Gardening Village," at www.naturalland.com. May 1997.

Powell, Eileen. *From Seed to Bloom: How to Grow Over 500 Annuals, Perennials and Herbs.* Garden Way Publishing, 1995.

Robbins, Weier, and John Stocking. *Botany: An Introduction to Plant Science.* Wiley & Sons, 1966.

Smith, Shane. *Greenhouse Gardener's Companion.* Fulcrum, 1992.

Toothill, Elizabeth and Stephen Blackmore, eds. *The Facts on File Dictionary of Botany.* Market House Books Ltd., 1984.

Turner, Carole B. *Seed Sowing and Saving.* Storey Publishing, 1998.

For listings of seed sources, try:

Barton, Barbara J. *Gardening by Mail, A Source Book.* Houghton Mifflin Co., 1997.

Feeney, Stephanie. *The Northwest Gardeners' Resource Directory, Seventh Edition.* Cedarcroft Press, 1997.

Index

About the Author

Linda D. Harris is a graduate of Temple University's School of Horti–culture and Landscape Design. Throughout her 25-year career she has worked continuously in the field of horticulture. Linda is currently a McCracken County Master Gardener and a horticultural writer and catalog designer for a seed company in Fulton, Kentucky, where she also gardens and writes a gardening column for the local newspaper.